Where Do I Fit?

Women in Ministry and Church Leadership

Work Book

Sandra Riley

Where Do I Fit? Women in Ministry and Church
Leadership

Copyright © 2019 by Sandra Riley

Dedication

This book is dedicated to my father,

the late Mr. Roy L. Thomas,

who encouraged me to become the leader I am

today.

Acknowledgments

I wouldn't be who I am if I did not first acknowledge my Lord and Savior Jesus Christ: the giver of all grace, love and truth, the creator of all knowledge. He has kept me and loved me every day of my life, and without Him I would be nothing.

Writing a book about women in leadership would have been impossible if not for the women who came before me, who paved the way for me to find my fit. Thank you to every woman who came before me for allowing your ceiling to be my floor.

Finally, to my team who helped review and edit this book. I appreciate you so much. I could not have done this without you. And a very special thank you to Jordan Brooks-Adams for your assistance in making this book come to life.

Table of Contents

ONE

WOMEN OF *Influence*

For those of you going through this workbook, you may find yourself in this place because there is some type of leadership component in you. Maybe you are already fully walking in your leadership capacity, and just looking to learn more. Or maybe you are developing it, birthing into it, trying to find your place in this complex and sometimes crazy leadership world. Where ever you are on your leadership journey, this workbook is for you.

The question we often come across as women in ministry and church leadership is *"Where Do I Fit?"* Often it's hard to figure out where we fit in our positions of leadership in the church, in work, and our communities. However, it's important we remember that women in church leadership are *problem solvers*. We are influential. We possess the spirit of influence—which is the capacity to impact people's thoughts, behaviors and beliefs. As such, Women of Influence impact our churches, our communities, our work places. And having influence is tied intrinsically to leadership.

In order to discover and develop who we are as Women of Influence in ministry and church leadership, we must ask the right questions. What is the next right, or God ordained move for your life? Not just any move! No. Nor can we be stuck where we are. But the next move has to be the perfect, God-ordained move for the next place in your life. But it takes courage. It takes courage that we really walk in leadership, especially as a woman in ministry and church leadership. It takes courage to stand in your truth and own who you are and what God has called you to do. And it takes asking the right questions.

This workbook has been designed to help guide you through the process of walking in courage as a woman in leadership and answering those questions. Each chapter has been divinely inspired to provide you with insight into who you are and where God wants you to go, by exploring phenomenal women of the Bible, and personal reflection questions to begin to dig deep into who you are as a leader. By the end of this book you will have a stronger idea of where **you** fit as a woman in leadership and what God is calling for you to do next!

THE COURAGE TO *Know*

"Being confident of this very thing, that He which hath begun a good work in you will perform it until the day of Jesus Christ"

Philippians 1:6 (KJV)

One of the most important things on this journey of leadership for us women is to know **who we are**! It is critical that you know you, and you are sure in who you are. Indeed, how can you know where you fit as a woman in leadership if you aren't sure of who you even are? However, once you are sure in who you are, you are empowered to know God's plan for your life and where God wants to take you and develop you as a leader.

Although I'm sure you're thinking: it's so easy to say "be sure of who you are," but how do you do that? Sometimes the best place to start with discovering who you are and what you are called to do is to start with **what you are passionate about**. The passions you have in your heart and mind are so important because they are what will *sustain* you on your leadership journey. When you are passionate, you will stick with it even when it gets rough. Even when it seems impossible, if it's really your passion, you have the courage to stick with it. So, God give us these things we are passionate about in order to discover who and what we are. Our passions are divinely connected to our purpose!

Sometimes discovering who you are and what you are called to do in the Kingdom of God may even start with taking a step backward and thinking about those things that you know you are *not* called to do. Maybe it's unclear about what God has designed for your life. And that's okay! But sometimes we are clear on what it isn't. We may not know where we fit, but we definitely know where we don't! And once we are able to identify those things we know aren't what God has designed for us, we can start removing things from our process from that point. But you have to have the courage to know and identify these things that we are even **not** called or purposed to do in order to get to the things God has designed for our lives.

Not only is it important to know who you are, and what you are called to do, but it's critical that we as women in leadership know and understand how God sees us! When we see ourselves how God sees us, we walk with purpose and authority and conviction throughout all parts of our lives. When we know how God values us, we don't take any part of our lives for granted. Nor do we let any one else take us for granted either. And when we know how God sees us, we understand our value as women and as leaders.

Don't be discouraged! The journey to knowing who you are takes time and patience and reexamining yourself and how God sees you over and over throughout the journey of life. But it is a worthwhile journey, especially for women in leadership. However, once we know who we are, we must guard that knowledge.

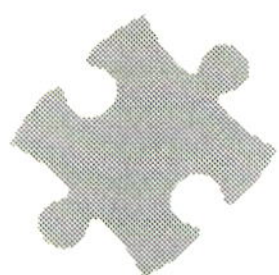

Now let's put some of this in practice. Take some time to think through these questions and answer them honestly on your journey as a woman in leadership.

What am I called to do? _______________________

____

____

____

What problem am I on earth to solve? __________

____

____

____

What am I passionate about? __________________

____

____

____

What vision does God have for my life? _________

____

____

____

What are some things that I am doing that are distracting me from what I'm meant to be doing? __________________________________

____

____

What are some things I am not called to do that I

am still doing anyway? ____________________________

____

____

____

How can I remove those things from my life? ____

____

____

____

____

The Shunammite Woman

II Kings 4:8 - 37

The Shunammite Woman in the book of II Kings is a powerful story of a woman who had the *Courage to Know* who she was as a woman and leader. Elisha encounters the Shunammite Woman as he travels to Shunam, and she greets him and cares for him with warm and overwhelming hospitality. She cared for the prophet as an honored guest, even though she was woman of wealth, a leader in her own right who ultimately possessed a servant's heart. She had wealth, riches, land, and people who answered to her. She knew who she was, and was confident in the woman she grew to be.

The prophet Elisha is overwhelmed by the generosity shown to him. As a result, he felt compelled to inquire what he could do for this Shunammite as a means of extending his gratitude and thanks. However, her answer was not what he was expecting. She told Elisha that she was sufficient in herself, and she had need for nothing. As a woman of courage, you have to know who you are, and be sure of what you already possess.

Although this woman was content in who she was, Elisha discovered that she didn't have a son, which was her true heart's desire. As a result, the man of God declared to the Shunammite woman that by that time the next year, she would have a son. Once the word was spoken, she knew that what was spoken was too serious to be a joke. Therefore, the Shunammite woman pleaded with the prophet to not lie or deceive her because having a son was too important to her.

Elisha's word was true, and she did conceive just as Elisha prophesied. However, though the promise manifested, the son did die an early death. When this occurred the Shunammite woman searched for the prophet and said to him, "I didn't ask for a son. You promised me that I would have a son. I was fine with my life as it was. But, you gave me a word, and I told you not to lie to me." After Elisha heard the heart of the Shunammite woman, God used him to perform a miracle in resurrecting her son.

My sister, hear me out. You may feel that you're facing a situation contrary to the promise God gave you. But, I want to remind you that God will not allow things to end as they currently are. You must have the courage to know that what God spoke over your life will not only come to pass, but it will also prosper.

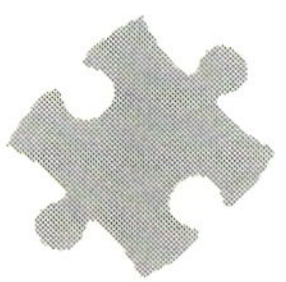

Has God ever given you a promise? Especially one connected to your purpose? What promises? _______________________________________

____

____

How has it felt when the promise was delayed?

____

____

____

How can you persevere despite how the delay

may feel? _______________________________

____

____

The Shunnamite Woman declared all was well

before she even received her promise—how can

you declare all is well in your life? _____________

____

____

THREE

THE COURAGE TO *Be*

"And those He predestined, He also called; those He called, He also justified; those He justified, He also glorified."

Romans 8:30 (NIV)

The bravest thing you can do as a woman in leadership in your church, your job or your community is to **walk in the truth and knowledge of who you are, who God called you to be, and to walk in your purpose.** Knowing who you are is just the first step on this long journey of leadership. And once you know and are sure of who you are and what God has purposed for your life, now begins the road to **be** that woman.

It's one thing to know your value, and another to make sure you don't offer anyone a discount on accessing the power and potential in you!

Often times we start to see the seeds of what God has put in us coming to life long before we even are conscious of what purpose He has called us to. Those seeds are shown in the way you can influence others, how they might take your advice, or seek your counsel. Perhaps even as a child you were able to guide other children.

These are all seeds of leadership God has placed in you, which are your responsibility to develop. You were wired for your purpose long before you even knew it! And now you can look back over your life and see how God was growing you and molding you into the powerful woman of God you are today. Knowing who and what you are called to do will not only help you understand why you have been wired the way you are—why you act or think the way you do—but will also help build the courage to accept the calling on your life to be a woman of influence and leadership.

All of the rough patches, road bumps, obstacles, pitfalls, joys and successes have been designed to help you realize your gifting and potential. God has provided you with all you need in your life to fulfill your purpose. Whatever resources you may think you don't have, God has given you the tools and ability to access them.

Yet, in order to really fulfill the promise of God, the purpose of God, in your life, **_you have to be you!_** Walk with power and authority in who God has designed you to be. As a leader, it can be hard to have the courage to be the woman God has called you to be. We often face criticism from all sides—family, friends, co-workers, church members, and even people we don't know! It is hard to face so much criticism from people who you don't know, and who don't know you—and still stay confident in who God has called you to be.

But you must remind yourself and others that **they don't write the dictionary that defines who you are.** Only God defines you. Only God created you. And only God called you to this place of leadership and effectiveness in your life. And when God defines who you are, it doesn't matter what anyone else says or believes about you. When the hand of the Lord is upon you, no one can beat you doing what He's called you to do.

Ultimately, success is not in how much money you have or how big your house is or how expensive your car is. Ultimately, success is doing what God has called you to do and being the woman that God has designed you to be. Success comes in yielding to the call and purpose on your life to impact the world as a woman of God, and to flourish as a leader. And when you measure your success according to God's yard stick, and not the world's, you won't be bothered by any negative comments or what anyone has to say about you. The key to finding the courage to be the leader God has designed you to be is to measure your success by God!

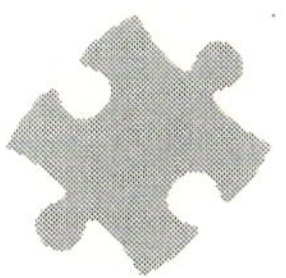

Let's put this into practice. Think about the woman God has called you to be, and how you can be sure and confidant in who you are.

What seeds of leadership has God placed in my life? ____

____

____

How does who I am make me a good leader? __

____

What are the skills and gifts God has given me?

____

____

What are my strengths? _______________________

____

____

My weaknesses? _______________________

____

____

How has God defined me? _______________________

____

____

How have I influenced other people? _______________________

____

____

Mary

Matthew 1:18 - 25; Luke 1:26 - 31

What do you do when the purpose God gives you causes your life to be put under a microscope? Mary, the mother of Jesus, is a great example of the Courage to Be who God called her to be despite what people said about her. Mary is at the prime of her life and preparing for a beautiful future when her life is interrupted with a message from God sent by the angel Gabriel telling her that she was chosen to carry within her womb the savior, Jesus Christ. But how, when she was a virgin? Can you imagine the shock that Mary experienced to be caught off guard with a word that would entirely alter the course of a future she was preparing for?

What has God told you that seemed too extreme for even you to believe? Have you experienced being pushed to the edge by knowing what God was producing in you? Mary was divinely picked to handle such a powerful task of birthing the savior of the world. However, the judgement and scrutiny she faced was so severe that even her husband wanted to divorce her!

It took another divine intervention from God, through the angel Gabriel as the messenger, to change Joseph's mind. But imagine—Mary's life was crumbling around her because of the divine purpose on her life! Yet, Mary had an assignment from God that she was committed to fulfilling, despite the consequences. Mary was committed to being the Woman God called her to be.

You have also been chosen by God to execute purpose that no one else can accomplish except you. Regardless of how others may look at you, or what their opinions may be of you, never lose sight of who you are, and who God has called you to be. You must be dedicated to God's purpose for your life. If not, by failing to be who you were called to be, you may be aborting what God has given you to birth.

What strength did Mary show in her courage to be? _______________________________________

____

____

What has God birthed in you that may be

aborted if you are not the woman God called

you to be? ____________________________________

____

____

How can you overcome fear of public opinion to

walk in your God ordained truth? _______________

____

____

What lessons can you learn from Mary's courage

to be who God called her to be? _______________

____

____

THE COURAGE TO *Believe*

"Trust in the Lord with all your heart and lean not on your own understanding; in all your ways submit to him, and he will make your paths straight."

Proverbs 3:5-6 (NIV)

What do you do when you know what God has called you to do, you know His purpose for your life, but it seems crazy—even to yourself? I know, it's hard! There are some dreams and passions that God gives us that we can't help but think, "God, what are you doing? I can't do this! I'm just me!" Still, the dream won't go away. The passion won't die. You think about this big "God-idea" all the time.

As a woman in leadership, it can sometimes seem really hard to believe what we know God has told us to do, even when we are sure it came from God. It is also sometimes hard even to believe that we are capable of being that leader that He has called us to be. It can be really difficult to believe in yourself and the effectiveness of your gift. That doubt is natural, but you can't get lost in it! Instead, you have to take control of your life and your doubts. Remind yourself over and over again about what you know God has called you to do, even if it seems impossible.

Once you know, and you walk in it, you also walk in confidence in that belief because you know the God in whom you believe, and the God who gave you the gifts to complete the purpose over your life. One of the most powerful things about God is that when He calls you to a task, He doesn't leave you in that place empty handed. But He empowers you to do the job! God won't bring you to a place that 1) He hasn't prepared you for, and 2) He hasn't prepared for you! When you know the call on your life, and begin walking in confidence, sometimes it's a daily journey to remind yourself that God is walking with you in leadership.

However, you have to be mindful of the words that you speak over yourself every single day.

When you say "I can't do it" or "that's impossible", you are speaking those doubts over your life. You are prophesying over your destiny. And its a dangerous thing to prophecy negativity over your destiny, because then you run the risk that you may never be the woman God has called you to be.

Also, be mindful of the conversations you allow yourself to be surrounded by. You can't get caught up in the conversations of pessimistic people, whose negativity will only drag on your spirit. Even watch the people around you who are insecure. You can't surround yourself with insecure people who only make you doubt yourself and what God told you!

Rather, surround yourself with people who are positive and confident, who speak positively in conversation. It may seem really tough, because sometimes our worst critics are our family and friends. And it hurts the worst when its the ones we love who don't seem to support us. But if God gave you the vision, you can't let anyone stop it. Not even your family!

The purpose God has placed in your life might seem impossible, but God has already empowered you and prepared you to do it. All He's asking is that you trust Him and believe.

Now let's put this into practice. Think about some of the ways in which you can work on your own belief in God, your purpose, and yourself as a woman in leadership.

What is the "impossible" idea God has given me to complete? ___________________________________

____

____

What are some steps I can take toward making that idea happen? ___________________________________

____

____

What has caused me to doubt the gifts God has placed in me? ___________________________________

____

____

How can I separate myself from the opinions of

others? _______________________________________

____

____

What are some positive words I can speak over

my own life every day? _________________________

____

____

Who are some positive people in my life I can

surround myself with? __________________________

____

____

Where Did She Fit?

Hannah

I Samuel 1:1 - 21

Your faith in God to fulfill that desire of your heart isn't truly tested until it has had to face adversity. Hannah exemplifies a woman with such clear and consistent belief in God. Hannah was one of the wives of a man named Elkanah. Unlike his other wife, Peninnah, Hannah had no children. Though she had no children, Elkanah loved Hannah dearly, and took great care of her. Hannah knew she was loved, yet she still felt inadequate because the Lord had shut up her womb.

As a result of Hannah's barrenness, Peninnah mocked her. And she provoked Hannah so much so until she wept bitterly from her soul because she felt unworthy of love and as if she was less of a woman and a wife. But, Hannah resolved in herself to seek the Lord and to petition him for a son. Hannah promised the Lord that if He would do this thing for her, she would dedicate her son's life fully to Him as an offering.

Eli saw Hannah praying and thought that maybe she was intoxicated because she expressed her heart to God with no sound coming out of her mouth, except the movement of her lips. Nevertheless, Hannah explained that she wasn't drunk, but rather was seeking the Lord for something she was desperate to receive. For this reason, God not only heard Hannah, but He answered her and she did give birth to a son whose name was Samuel, a prophet of God. The amazing thing about Hannah's story is that the depth of her belief was so great, that in giving up her heart's desire, her son Samuel, by returning him to the Lord, He multiplied His blessings in her life. The Lord gave her what she asked for and more! After Samuel, Hannah went on to birth three sons and two daughters.

Many of us have felt like Hannah—comparing ourselves to others, and feeling inadequate as women in leadership because of what we thought we were unable to produce. However, you must have the courage to believe God like never before! When you take the step to believe God to fulfill His promises and purpose in your life, like Hannah, He will give you more than you ever

asked or believed.

What are you believing God to do in your life that

seems impossible? _______________________________

____

____

How have you stood strong in the face of people

you love who don't understand your faith? _______

____

____

Hannah was constantly provoked to doubt by

her husband's other wife, but still kept her faith in

God. What are some ways you can continue to

believe when giving up seems easier?

46

____

____

____

How has Hannah's story inspired you to fight

doubt in your life? _______________________

____

____

THE COURAGE TO *Work*

"What good is it, my brothers and sisters, if you say you have faith but do not have works?"

James 2:14 (NRSV)

Everyone wants to be a leader, but few people want to put in the work. Don't let anyone fool you: leadership takes work. It takes time, commitment, sacrifice, long hours, and patience. Leadership is much bigger than just being in charge of others. Having and executing vision requires investment, research, and time. Above all, you must work on yourself as much as you work on the purpose and dream God has given you.

As a leader, it is critical that you work on yourself consistently. Working on yourself means understanding that any investment you make in yourself is not a selfish thing, but a means of growth! By working on yourself, you make yourself a better leader. As a better leader, you are more capable of handling and completing the purpose God has placed on your life. Regardless of your area of leadership, you should constantly invest in yourself and the work you are doing.

One of the simplest ways to invest in yourself is to know about those who are doing the same work as you. If you are a preacher, you should know who some of the most relevant and anointed preachers are. If you are an educator, you should know who are the prominent educators in your field. This goes for other fields, including music, law, design, creatives, entrepreneurs. You name it. Following the major leaders in your field and gifting arena is important because they are people who have established effective leadership styles. Knowing who they are, and how they are effective, may give you inspiration on how to further develop your own gift.

Additionally, invest in information that will help you perfect your skills. Whether its studying books, watching informative videos online, or attending conferences and training sessions—it is important to develop and cultivate your gifting and skills by gaining knowledge and insight from those who have already established themselves as successful leaders in your area of gifting.

As women in leadership, we are constantly put in positions of having to prove ourselves as leaders who are capable, intelligent, and rational—especially against these stereotypes that argue that women can't be as effective in leadership as men. Let's be honest... the glass ceiling for women in leadership exists in the church as much as it does in the corporate world! So, this is where your Courage to Work has to kick in high gear.

Your courage to work, to invest in this dream and purpose God has given you, cannot be limited to just investing in yourself and working on yourself, but also making the commitment to work on the purpose and plan God has for your life. Stick to it when it gets rough, when the money seems low, when people aren't supporting you. Be diligent in the assignment God has given you, and when you do, He will take you to the next level and the next level and the next.

We have to have the courage to work hard despite the adversity we may face as leaders. Also, we must have the courage to face our own work, gifts and skills, and examine what we have been doing well and what we may need to improve upon. You may already feel like your own worst critic. That is okay. It will make you a better leader. But don't forget to believe in and invest in yourself, so that you can be your own biggest fan.

Now let's put this into practice. Think through how you can invest in yourself, and how you can either start or improve upon the work that you are already doing for your purpose.

What are 3 things I can start today to work on myself? __________________________________

____

____

____

Who are the major players in my field? _________

____

____

What are they doing that I admire? ______________

____

____

____

What are they doing that I would change? ______

____

____

____

What are 3 steps I can take to move my purpose

forward this year? ______________________________

____

____

____

How can I start making these 3 steps happen?

____

____

How can I improve what I am already doing?

Lydia

Acts 16:14 - 15; 40

Although she is not heavily mentioned in scripture, theologians and Biblical scholars believe a woman by the name of Lydia played a critical role in the foundation of the early Christian church. The bible teaches us that she was an entrepreneur and business woman, with her own successful business in selling fine dyed cloth. Lydia also was in an unusual position as head of her own household, and provided the financial stability to support servants and those others who lived with her.

Paul and Silas first encounter Lydia in the city center, where she is among a group of women gathering for the Sabbath. As the only woman mentioned by name in that group, Lydia probably served as a community leader as well as successful business woman. Yet, she is described as being a worshipper at heart, and it is her love for God that plants the seed of conversion upon hearing the message of Paul and Silas.

Lydia's impact as a woman of influence was so powerful that when she decided to be baptized and receive Christ, her entire household followed her conversion. She continued to be a religious leader for the new converts even after meeting Paul and Silas, until it was to Lydia's house that

Paul and Silas went after their release from prison. She was not only financially able to support Paul and Silas as guests until the next phase of their journey, but there were many fellow believers in Christ at her house who were there when Paul and Silas arrived. Arguably, Lydia worked so hard for the body of Christ that her own home served as the meeting place for the first church community in Philippi.

What kind of woman Lydia must have been to cause her family, household, and community to follow her example? Do you not realize that you have been given influence to change the culture of the world around through the decisions you make? Lydia, was so confident in who she was and didn't mind working with her talents and skills. And, as a result, God blessed her and granted her, and her family, favor. Like Lydia, it is important for you to remember that the only way that your dreams and purpose can come into fruition is when you have the courage to work. Work your dream. Work your vision. Work your passion. Work your gifts. Now is the time to work!

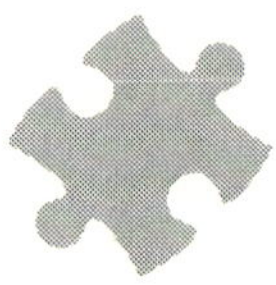

What are three ways you can influence your household and community for your purpose like Lydia? ___________________________________

____

____

Lydia balanced life as a business woman and Church influencer. How can you practice balance in your life? ________________________

____

____

Lydia's courage to work for Christ may have been risky because she was a Roman citizen. What risks are you willing to take for the call on your life? ________________________

____

____

How has Lydia's story encouraged you to find the Courage to Work for what God has called you to do? ________________________

____

____

____

THE COURAGE TO *Change*

"Therefore, if anyone is in Christ, he is a new creation; old things have passed away; behold, all things have become new."
2 Corinthians 5:17 (NKJV)

Change is possibly the hardest thing to do as a human, never mind in leadership! In fact, change seems almost contrary to our human nature. Yet, change—or the ability to adapt to your shifting environment and shifting needs—is a critical component to effective leadership.

As leaders, we must be willing to ask the tough questions of ourselves, our processes, and those we lead, and find out what worked and what didn't work. There is this misconception that having to go back to the drawing board to redevelop your idea or strategy means failure. No! It simply means that the idea wasn't the one you really needed. And it gives you an opportunity to know what doesn't work.

Just like earlier, where we talked about knowing what you're not called to do, the process of change is about learning what didn't work for the need you have. In the process of discovering where you fit, you also discover which methods and ideas fit into the purpose and plan God has for your life.

But when you are working on yourself and the purpose God has for your life, but you don't like what you see, how do you change it? It seems so easy to just say change it. But **how?**

First, you have to be willing to let go of the past. Whether its past hurts, past experiences, past mistakes, past missteps, past stumbles, past obstacles, or past heart break. You have to let it go. If you don't let go of them, then they will continue to weigh on you and you can never climb to the heights God has called you to. Whether it was a relationship, a job, school, or an idea—don't relive it! In order for roses to grow, the plant surrounding them must be trimmed.

Change also requires honesty: with yourself and your situation. You must be honest about where you are at in your place of leadership, as well as emotionally, physically and mentally. As women in leadership, we have to be careful and guard our hearts and minds, and be willing to be honest if we are not where we should be.

Even more, we should be honest about what methods and ideas didn't work. If the business plan, program, or job didn't work, let it go and move forward. But in the process of letting it go, be critical about what didn't work, so that you don't repeat the same mistakes.

The most important thing in change is to remember this: Raise the Standard. When you move forward in life, raise the standard. Continue to grow, develop, and evolve **forward**. Raising the standard is about allowing your perspective to change as God moves you forward into your purpose. It means having the Courage to Work toward the purpose God has placed on your life!

Now let's put it into practice. Think about the ways in which God is pushing you to change in your role as a leader.

What am I doing well in my leadership role?

____

____

____

What can I work on? _______________________

____

____

____

What am I still doing that doesn't seem to be

working? ________________________________

____

____

What in my past am I holding on to?

____

____

____

What steps can I take to let it go?

____

____

____

What can I do to move forward?

____

____

____

What can I do to Raise the Standard? _________

____

____

____

Rahab
Joshua 2

The wall was huge and impenetrable, surrounding the city of Jericho. Though the Israelites knew the Lord had brought them through many victories, this one seemed almost impossible. And nestled in the wall was the home of Rahab, the harlot, or prostitute. In a way, Rahab was an excellent business woman, such that even the King knew her by name. However, her success and business skills were misguided and the result of her negative choices and misdirected values.

Yet, when she was met by the Israelite spies, she made a conscious decision that changed her trajectory, and ultimately her life. It was in her house that two men of Israel hid when their attempts to spy on the land where discovered by the King. She saved their lives by hiding them on her roof and sending those after them in the wrong direction. Though her life had been built on bad choices, she built up enough courage to change and saved their lives when she could have easily given them away.

What's so amazing about Rahab is that she had heard of the God of Israel, and His miracles and power. Sometimes, my sister, as leaders we know the right thing, but find ourselves doing the opposite anyway. However, God still gives us the opportunity to do better and change even when we have made bad decisions! As a result of her help, the Israelite spies not only made it safely out of the city, but she played a key role in the Israelites' victory against Jericho.

Even more, since she had the Courage to Change despite pressure from even her own ruler, the Lord spared her life, the lives of her family, and her home in the destruction of the wall and conquering of the city. But you know the greatest part of this story? Rahab, once viewed as an ungodly woman who worshiped pagan gods and sold her body for money, became a part of the lineage of Jesus. When you have the courage to change as a woman in leadership, God can change any circumstance or bad decision you have made and set you on the right path to impact a generation and change the world.

What lesson can you learn from Rahab?

____

____

____

____

How did Rahab display Courage to Change despite her circumstances? _______________

____

____

____

How can you turn your past mistakes into a testimony? _______________________________

____

71

____

____

What do you think God is seeking from you to

change? ______________________________________

____

____

____

PUTTING IT ALL *Together*

If there is one thing you should remember in the process of discovering where you fit and developing your skills and gifting as a Woman of Leadership, it is that leadership does not happen overnight. It takes time, effort, mistakes, and failures in order to truly cultivate the purpose for which God has designed your life.

Most importantly, it takes courage. Finding out where you fit in leadership is not for the faint of heart. When you are faced with the daunting question of "Where Do I Fit?", things may start to seem overwhelming and confusing. But God has given you the tools, knowledge and resources in order to not only find your place, but your perfect, God-ordained fit.

This work book has been designed to help you think through the process of both discovering, and implementing, the leadership component in you. God designed you to be a woman of influence long before you ever stepped into leadership in your community, church, or job. In order to truly walk in your place as a leader, you must have the courage to **KNOW** who you are, **BE** the woman God called you to be, **BELIEVE** in what God has given you, **WORK** for your purpose, and **CHANGE** when you need to change.

Keep this work book with you as you continue on your leadership journey and revisit your answers when you can, even answering them over again through every new season. Let your answers be a reminder of your growth and goals. And remember: despite the difficulties you may face as Women in Leadership, even encountering your own glass ceilings, when God has called you to a purpose, He has already empowered you to succeed. You will find where you fit.

ABOUT THE *Author*

Pastor Sandra Riley, conference speaker, Talk Show host, seminar presenter, women and young adult workshop presenter, is one of the nations most highly sought after conference speakers who has obtained national and international acclaim across denominational lines.

As President and CEO of "Just for U Ministries," Sandra Riley has been touched by the hand of God and has received keen insight into what God speaks to this generation. Sandra Riley's passion for the depth and heights of God causes her to operate in the highest level of excellence in ministry. She possesses an unusual in-depth understanding of the Holy Word of God and is able to effectively exegete the meaning a biblical text had for its original hearers into the application it has for believers of this time and culture.

Sandra was ordained minister at the Bethel Pentecostal Church Abundant Life Center, in Grand Rapids, Michigan under the Pastorate of the late Bishop William C. Abney. She is presently an Associate Pastor at New Life Covenant Church Southeast, under the leadership of Pastor John F. Hannah. As an accomplished businesswoman Sandra has served as

President and CEO of Rabah Group LLC, Inc., a real estate investment company specializing in rentals to low-income families.

Sandra Riley can be seen every Saturday afternoon at 6:30p.m. EST on The Word Network where she hosts Just For U with Sandra Riley. She is featured in First Family Film's documentary of women in ministry entitled "Every Soldier Counts" and the African American Pulpit Journal named Sandra one of the "Emerging Voices" who will shape the future of the African American Church. Sandra travels across the U.S. and abroad conducting seminars, workshops and conferences addressing issues that impact youth, singles, women and men. Her approach reflects her sensitivity to the needs of God's people, emphasizing that this is a ministry "Just For U."

Made in the USA
Middletown, DE
24 October 2022

13345668R00047